POST BREAKUP TO DO LIST

Revenge is a dish best served cold

1 BUY WINE

Drink wine

2 PENS, PENCILS, CRAYONS

Grab your coloring supplies together

3 COLOR

Color your ex out of your life

4 YOU ARE BETTER OFF

Now go back to step one and have fun

POST ON FACEBOOK AND SHARE ON INSTAGRAM @CREATIVECOLLECTIVE

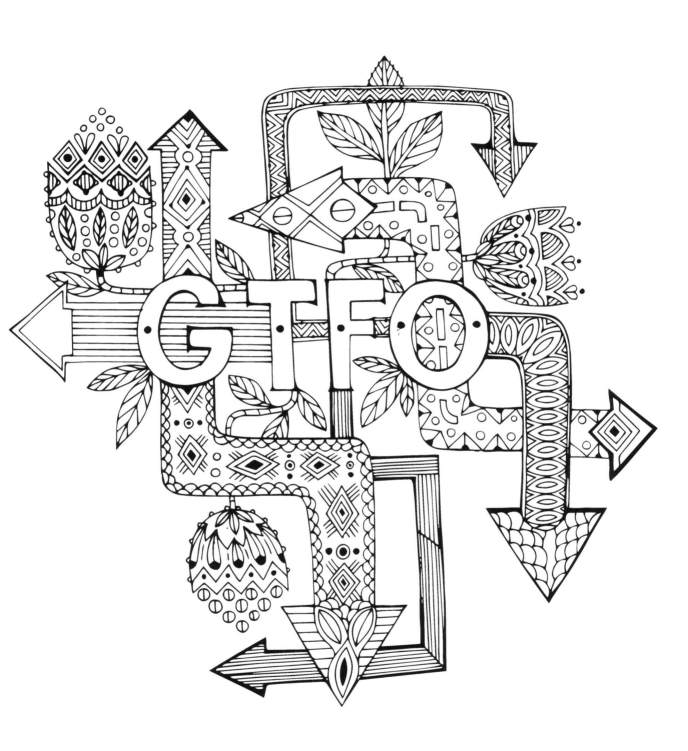

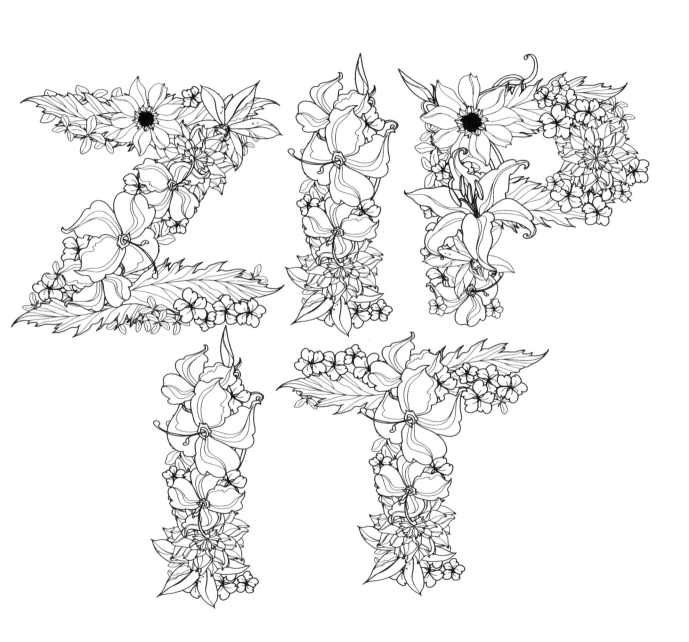

Made in the USA
San Bernardino, CA
05 February 2020